P9-DEP-087

THE SELMA MARCHES FOR CIVIL RIGHTS

We Shall Overcome

BY STEVEN OTFINOSKI

MATTESON AREA PUBLIC LIBRARY
DISTRICT

Consultant:
Richard Bell, PhD
Associate Professor of History
University of Maryland, College Park

CAPSTONE PRESS
a capstone imprint

Tangled History is published by Capstone Press,
1710 Roe Crest Drive, North Mankato, Minnesota 56003
www.mycapstone.com

Copyright © 2019 by Capstone Press, a Capstone imprint. All rights reserved. No part of
this publication may be reproduced in whole or in part, or stored in a retrieval system,
or transmitted in any form or by any means, electronic, mechanical, photocopying,
recording, or otherwise, without written permission of the publisher.

Library of Congress Cataloging-in-Publication data
Names: Otfinoski, Steven, author.
Title: The Selma marches for civil rights : we shall overcome / by Steven Otfinoski.
Description: North Mankato, Minnesota : Capstone Press, [2019]
Series: Tangled history | Audience: 008-014.
Identifiers: LCCN 2018012341 (print) | LCCN 2018013425 (ebook)
ISBN 9781515779698 (eBook PDF)
ISBN 9781515779414 (hardcover)
ISBN 9781515779650 (pbk.)
Subjects: LCSH: Civil rights movements—Alabama—Selma—History—20th
century—Juvenile literature. | African Americans—Civil rights—United
States—History—20th century—Juvenile literature. | African Americans—Suffrage—
United States—History—20th century—Juvenile literature.
Classification: LCC F334.S4 (ebook) | LCC F334.S4 O895 2019 (print)
DDC 323.1196/0730904—dc23
LC record available at https://lccn.loc.gov/2018012341

Editorial Credits
Adrian Vigliano, editor; Bobbie Nuytten, designer; Jo Miller, media researcher;
Kathy McColley, production specialist

Photo Credits
AP Images: 56, Bill Achatz, 105; Getty Images/Bettmann/Contributor, cover, 13, 17, 20,
31, 45, 62, 66, 70, 80, 83, Frank Dandridge/Contributor, 37, MPI/Stringer, 8, PhotoQuest/
Contributor, 40, Stephen F. Somerstein/Contributor, 97; Newscom: BlackStar Photos/Flip
Schulke, 48, Everett Collection, 7, 28, 85, 95, 99, KRT/Gabriel B. Tait, 103, ZUMA Press/
Contra Costa Times/Eddie Ledesma, 25, ZUMA Press/Kns Archive, 4; Shutterstock:
olgers, cover (news print background); Wikimedia: Lyndon Baines Johnson Library and
Museum/Yoichi Okamoto, 90

Printed in the Canada.
PA020

TABLE OF CONTENTS

Civil rights activists around the United States began sitting in protest at whites-only lunch counters in 1960.

FOREWORD

By 1965 the modern-day fight for the civil rights
of African Americans was entering its 10th year.
During that time, the Southern Christian Leadership
Conference (SCLC), led by Martin Luther King Jr., had
fought Southern institutional racism and discrimination.

It had done so using nonviolent demonstrations, sit-ins, and marches. King found an unlikely but powerful ally in the new president, Lyndon Baines Johnson. Through their combined efforts, King and Johnson had gotten Congress to pass the Civil Rights Act of 1964, which made racial discrimination in employment and public facilities illegal.

But African Americans were still denied the right to vote in many parts of the South. Local and state governments made it extremely difficult for black citizens to register to vote. They gave unfair literacy tests that no one—black or white—could be expected to pass. They stopped black people from registering by threatening to tell prospective voters' employers that they had registered. This threat told black people that they would lose their jobs for registering to vote. Without the vote, black citizens had no voice in who would represent them in local, state, and national government.

Selma, in Dallas County, Alabama, had a large black population, but only 156 of the 15,000 black adults who lived there were registered to vote.

For this reason, in 1964, King chose Selma as a testing ground for voter registration demonstrations and protests. Over the next several months, both outside activists and local residents protested at the county courthouse on the issue of voter registration. Among the hundreds of demonstrators arrested on February 1 was King himself. While in jail, King wrote his stirring "A Letter from a Selma, Alabama, Jail." The letter appeared in *The New York Times* on February 5, 1965, the day he was released on bail.

On February 28 a public meeting was held following the death of Jimmie Lee Jackson. Jackson, a black man, had marched in a peaceful protest in Marion, Alabama, on February 18. Alabama state troopers attacked the marchers and shot Jackson. He died eight days later. At the February 28 meeting, SCLC leader James Bevel suggested that King lead a march from Selma to Montgomery. Once in Montgomery, the capital of Alabama, King would directly confront Governor George Wallace about Jackson's death. King approved of the march, but he was worried about attacks on marchers by Alabama state troopers and white racists.

Martin Luther King Jr. (left) along with fellow SCLC leaders Ralph Abernathy (center) and Andrew Young (right) led a voter registration effort for black citizens in Selma, Alabama, on March 1, 1965.

King left Selma on Friday, March 5, with his second-in-command, Ralph Abernathy. He planned to lead Sunday services in his home church in Atlanta, Georgia. Then he would return to Selma later on Sunday and lead the march.

"GOD, WE'RE BEING KILLED!"

1

George Wallace

George Wallace

State Capitol, Montgomery, Alabama,
March 6, 1965, 9:00 a.m.

Alabama Governor George Wallace was beginning to lose the self-confidence that had made him a national political figure. In 1963 he had vowed, "Segregation today, segregation tomorrow, segregation forever." His strict stand on racial segregation had made him a popular leader with many white people in the South. But Wallace had been unable to stop Martin Luther King Jr.'s civil rights demonstrations in Selma. This had seriously challenged Wallace's authority.

Under Wallace's orders, men such as Dallas County Sheriff Jim Clark had responded to the civil rights activists. They had beaten demonstrators with clubs and sent electric shocks through them with cattle prods. But this had earned the governor unfavorable news headlines.

Wallace didn't want more bad publicity if King followed through with his plan to march from Selma to Montgomery the next day. Yet he also wanted to stop the march and demonstrate his authority. He didn't know what to do.

Wallace called a press conference and tried to appear in control. The march, he told the gathered reporters, could not be tolerated. He explained that the march would interrupt the orderly flow of traffic and commerce on State Highway 80.

After the conference ended, Wallace pulled aside state trooper Colonel Al Lingo. "Use whatever measures are necessary to prevent a march," he said.

A short time later Wallace spoke to Lingo's lieutenant, Major John Cloud. He warned Cloud not to take any actions that would cause sensationalism. "If they want to march, go beside them and protect them," Wallace said.

Cloud nodded, but the governor wondered what the troopers would do when the time came. He had a terrible feeling that events were still spinning out of his control.

Ralph Abernathy

West Hunter Baptist Church,
Atlanta, Georgia, March 7, 1965, 9:45 a.m.

The Reverend Abernathy was preparing for Sunday morning services when the phone rang. It was Hosea Williams, another SCLC leader in Selma. After hearing Wallace's press conference warning, King and Abernathy had decided to postpone the march. But Williams felt the moment for the march was right. He said that the civil rights activists who had come to Selma to demonstrate—both black and white—were ready. He requested that Abernathy ask King for permission to go ahead with the march to Montgomery in King's absence.

Abernathy didn't care much for Williams. He thought Williams was too eager for a fight and seemed too anxious to lead the march. King had affectionately called Williams "my wild man," but for Abernathy his wildness appeared reckless.

Yet Abernathy put aside his personal feelings and tried to consider what was best for the movement. He told Williams that he'd call King.

Abernathy reached King on the phone at his own church, Ebenezer Baptist, where he too was preparing to lead services. He told King about Williams' proposal to go ahead with the march. There was a long pause at the other end of the line.

"Do you think we ought to let him go ahead?" King asked.

Abernathy knew King valued his opinion and he didn't hesitate to give it. "If he wants to get his [behind] beaten, then let him do it," replied Abernathy. "Because if we don't, he'll blame us the rest of his life, saying he could have done this or that."

"Tell him he can go," King said.

Abernathy immediately called Williams back. "Hosea, go to it," he said.

"We're gone," shouted Williams into the phone.

Jim Clark

Sheriff Jim Clark looked at his deputies with pride as they flexed their clubs and whips. Then he looked at his clean shirt and the big button on it.

Jim Clark

The button bore just one word, "NEVER." It expressed Clark's feelings about integration in Dallas County. For months, Clark had backed up his words with action. He had ruthlessly beaten up and arrested both black and white demonstrators whom he felt disturbed the peace.

Yet all his efforts were unappreciated by the very man he was serving, Governor Wallace. Wallace had turned authority over to men like Al Lingo of the state troopers and Selma Police Chief Wilson Baker. Clark despised Baker. Baker was a segregationist, but soft on enforcing the law against these civil rights troublemakers. Now with the march only a few hours away, Clark had no intention of taking a back seat to anybody. While Lingo would be commanding his troopers, Clark had his posse—men who were loyal to him and him alone. Clark would show them all, including the governor, that he was a law-and-order man with whom to be reckoned.

Lynda Blackmon

Brown Chapel, Selma, Alabama,
March 7, 1965, 2:00 p.m.

Lynda Blackmon marched with her friends to Brown Chapel. This was where hundreds of people were gathering for the 54-mile march to Montgomery. At age 14, Blackmon was already a seasoned civil rights activist. In the last two years, she had marched with other black students and had been arrested and jailed nine times. She joined the movement after her grandmother took her to hear King speak when she was 13. He argued that the denial of voting rights to black people was preventing them from gaining their full rights as Americans. King's words had inspired her.

Blackmon had been looking forward to this day for weeks. She knew this would be the most important march of which she had yet been a part. She guessed there were already several hundred people gathered in the chapel. More were coming every few minutes.

This would be a day, Blackmon told herself, that she would remember for the rest of her life.

John Lewis

Selma, Alabama,
March 7, 1965, 4:00 p.m.

Twenty-five-year-old John Lewis adjusted the backpack on his shoulders and straightened his tie. The backpack contained a toothbrush, toothpaste, some fruit, and several books. He was marching to Montgomery wearing a suit, just like his hero, Martin Luther King Jr.

Lewis, a native Alabamian, was the son of sharecroppers. He had been working for civil rights since he was a college student at Fisk University in Nashville, Tennessee. He had helped found the Student Nonviolent Coordinating Committee (SNCC) and was its national chairman.

John Lewis (right) and Hosea Williams (left) led marchers
across the Edmund Pettus Bridge on March 7, 1965.

His activities in working to register black voters had
brought him to Selma, where he joined forces with
King's SCLC.

Now he and Hosea Williams were about to lead this important march together. Lewis was realistic about the day's probable outcome. Lawmen, under orders from Governor Wallace, were unlikely to let the march go very far before breaking it up. But there would be more marches and the marchers would, in the words of the old song, "overcome."

As they prepared to start for the Pettus Bridge, Lewis faced the gathered newspeople. He read a short statement to them about the purpose of the march. Next, everyone kneeled and Andrew Young, another of King's fellow leaders, said a prayer. Then they were off, marching two by two along the narrow walkway on the Pettus Bridge.

The bridge arced upward, spanning the muddy, still waters of the Alabama River. Lewis, in the lead with Williams, couldn't see the other side until they reached the crest of the bridge. When they reached the crest, the two men stopped dead at the sight before them. On the other end of the bridge stood a wall of blue-helmeted state troopers.

The troopers were brandishing nightsticks and canisters of what might be tear gas. Behind the troopers were Sherriff Jim Clark's men, some of them on horseback.

Lewis looked down at the waters about 100 feet below.

"John," Williams asked, "can you swim?"

"No," Lewis confessed.

"Well, neither can I," admitted Williams. "But we might have to."

They proceeded down the bridge to the bottom where it met Highway 80. One of the troopers stepped forward. Lewis recognized him as Major John Cloud.

"This march you propose is not conducive to public safety," Cloud said. "If you continue, it will be detrimental to your safety. You've got two minutes to turn around and go back to your church."

Lewis felt trapped. They couldn't go forward, and going back would be just as difficult, given the tight formation of the marchers. He thought about what King would do in these circumstances.

"We should kneel and pray," he said to the marchers. The word spread back through the long line. Some kneeled. Some lowered their heads.

"Troopers, advance," ordered Major Cloud.

Alabama state troopers moved in to violently stop civil rights marchers near the Pettus Bridge on March 7, 1965.

Lynda Blackmon

Edmund Pettus Bridge,
Selma, Alabama,
March 7, 1965, 4:15 p.m.

Blackmon was on her knees praying when she heard it—a strange popping sound. As she rose to her feet something in the air was burning her eyes. Her lungs hurt, so she couldn't breathe. It was tear gas.

All around her, people were yelling and crying. A trooper grabbed her from behind. She bit his hand and he struck her head twice. Her eyes still stinging from the tear gas, she ran a short distance and collapsed. The next thing she knew some men were lifting her onto a stretcher.

She leaped up and started running back across the bridge toward the safety of Brown Chapel.

John Lewis

Edmund Pettus Bridge, Selma, Alabama, March 7, 1965, 4:20 p.m.

Lewis stood his ground. A large trooper charged at him with a nightstick as long as a baseball bat. Lewis felt shooting pains as the club slammed into the left side of his head. Once. Twice. Blood streamed down into his eyes.

A cloud of tear gas filled the air, choking him. All around him people were running and stumbling, pursued by troopers and posse members. Some of the attackers were on foot and others on horseback. "God," he heard someone say, "we're being killed!"

Lewis saw one man lying on the median of the bridge, vomiting from the toxic tear gas. Mixed in with the cries and moans of the marchers were the cheers and whoops of white bystanders.

They were lined up along the bridge waving Confederate flags in open defiance of this struggle for civil rights.

Lynda Blackmon

Edmund Pettus Bridge, Selma, Alabama, March 7, 1965, 4:22 p.m.

As she reached the Selma side of the bridge, Blackmon saw a sight that made her blood run cold. A man was holding her little sister, Joanne, in his arms.

"Oh, she's dead. They killed my sister!" Blackmon cried.

But the man said she had only fainted. Blackmon slapped Joanne's face. She opened her eyes, stared at Blackmon, and screamed. Blackmon realized Joanne was reacting to her blood-covered face.

She grabbed Joanne's hand and they ran for Brown Chapel. When they saw a ring of troopers around the chapel they turned and ran for the First Baptist Church.

Jim Clark

Clark was ready. He led his posse down the bridge and into the heart of Selma's largest black neighborhood. He was prepared to pursue the marchers to the very doors of their redbrick apartments.

As Clark headed through the crowded streets, Selma Sheriff Wilson Baker confronted him. He told Clark to back off, that he was still in charge.

"I've already waited a month too long about moving in!" Clark replied, pushing past Baker. He ordered his men to keep after the fleeing marchers.

Violence against the marchers resulted in 17 being hospitalized and many others suffering injuries.

He even ordered them to toss tear gas canisters into one home he decided looked suspicious.

Some black people were fighting back, throwing bricks and bottles at the posse men. One rock nicked Clark.

The marchers eventually retreated and the situation finally quieted down. Baker approached Clark again. "Get your cowboys out of here," he said.

Clark frowned, but there wasn't much more to do. There was no one left to chase or beat up.

John Lewis

Brown Chapel, Selma,
Alabama, March 7, 1965, 8:00 p.m.

Wounded, weary, but still defiant, the marchers gathered at the chapel for a meeting. They needed to look back on the horrible events of this bloody Sunday. Lewis, still weak from the blows to his head, was one of them. Like many other marchers Lewis had received medical care at the chapel. It had resembled the emergency ward of a hospital. Now, despite the sharp pains in his head, Lewis prepared to speak and listen.

Hosea Williams spoke first to the crowd and then Lewis took the pulpit. Lewis blamed Governor Wallace for the violence, calling him a vicious and evil man. He went on to express disappointment that President Lyndon Johnson hadn't supported the march and protected the marchers.

"I don't see how he can send troops to Vietnam and can't send troops to Selma, Alabama," Lewis said. "Next time we march, we may have to keep going when we get to Montgomery. We may have to go on to Washington."

"AIN'T GONNA LET NOBODY TURN ME AROUND"

2

Martin Luther King Jr. addressed members of the media in Selma, Alabama.

The news of the brutal attack on the Selma marchers reached King late that afternoon. He was stunned by the violence against the marchers and angry that Governor Wallace had allowed it. He also felt a bit guilty that he hadn't been there.

By evening he was issuing statements to the press condemning the violence. He said the attack was "the lowest form of barbarity" and had taken place "under the sanction and authority of Governor Wallace."

He also resolved to lead a second march from Selma to Montgomery in two days. He began sending telegrams to ministers and other religious leaders nationwide. He asked them to come to Selma and join the second march.

The shocking violence of "Bloody Sunday," as it was now called, appeared on the news.

Would Wallace dare to repeat the violence knowing the world was watching? King didn't know. But he was determined not to let anything stop him in his struggle for voting rights.

Frank Johnson

Montgomery, Alabama,
March 8, 1965, 9:00 a.m.

Judge Frank Johnson looked down from his bench at the anxious faces of King's lawyers. He knew they were expecting a ruling that would allow King to lead a legal march on Tuesday. If Johnson's ruling was favorable it would prevent Governor Wallace from stopping the marchers with a restraining order.

The lawyers had every reason to expect a favorable ruling. Judge Johnson was sympathetic to civil rights activists and their cause. He was also a man of courage. The Ku Klux Klan, a racist hate group, had issued death threats against him and his family for his beliefs and actions.

Judge Frank Johnson

But given the events of "Bloody Sunday," Judge Johnson wanted to prevent further violence. He saw no reason to rush the marchers into another confrontation with Governor Wallace.

Looking down at the lawyers and the rest of the courtroom, Johnson gave his decision.

"This court does not see from the complaint . . . any justification for issuing a temporary restraining order without notice to the defendants and without a hearing," he declared. "There will be no irreparable harm if the plaintiffs will await a judicial determination of the matters involved."

Judge Johnson would see that King got his march, but he would have to wait for it. King's lawyers looked decidedly disappointed.

John Lewis

Good Samaritan Hospital, Selma, Alabama, March 8, 1965, 1:00 p.m.

Lewis wanted to be anywhere other than a hospital bed. But the doctors had diagnosed his injury as a fractured skull when he walked into the hospital after the Brown Chapel meeting. Lewis had been injured a number of times before in demonstrations and marches. But he had never been hurt so badly that he had to be admitted to a hospital.

The only good parts about it were the telegrams and letters he had received from friends and strangers alike. The most touching message, accompanied by a wreath, came from a woman in California. A FORMER ALABAMIAN, WE ARE WITH YOU, it read, in all capital letters.

All at once the door to his hospital room opened and in walked King and Ralph Abernathy. Lewis' face lit up in a smile. He was touched that they had taken time out of their busy schedules to visit him. They said how proud they were of him and his leadership in the march. They said they were as eager as he was to see him back working with them. When Lewis asked about the next march, King patted his shoulder.

"It's going to happen, John," King said softly. "Rest assured it is going to happen."

King looked out at the sea of eager faces in Brown Chapel, at the people waiting to hear his words. Religious leaders had come from as far away as Hawaii, answering King's call to join the march to Montgomery. That was heartening. What was disheartening was Judge Johnson's surprise restraining order not to march.

King faced a dilemma. If he disobeyed the order and marched, he would be defying the federal government. He might lose the support of President Johnson, who had been a firm backer of civil rights. If he obeyed the order and didn't march, he would disappoint the hundreds of supporters who had traveled so far to march with him.

Under pressure from the Justice Department and the president, who had not wanted him to march, King had agreed to a compromise.

He would begin the march and then end it before confronting Wallace's state troopers. This way he would avoid a repeat of the violence of "Bloody Sunday." It was a compromise that King didn't want to make, but he saw no other way. It would keep the movement alive while preventing physical harm to him and his followers. He had shared this decision with only a few people in his inner circle and that bothered him too. All his supporters deserved to know the truth. But King tried to put such thoughts out of his head as he began to speak to the crowd.

"Nothing will stop us, not the threat of death itself," he told the crowd. "The only way we can get our freedom is to have no fear of death. . . . We will not be turned around. The world must know that we are determined to be free."

The crowd roared its approval. His listeners seemed ready to follow him anywhere. And he would lead them to victory, he promised himself, but not today.

Ralph Abernathy

The sun was shining brightly, but the air was cold as the marchers moved out. Abernathy walked beside King, leading the group up Broad Street to the Pettus Bridge. At the foot of the bridge, a U.S. marshal was waiting for them, holding a copy of Judge Johnson's order. As they came to a halt, the marshal read the order.

"I am aware of the order," King said firmly.

The marshal looked at the long line of marchers and then looked at the bridge. "I am not going to interfere with this march," he said, speaking to his deputies. "Let them go."

Abernathy, who knew of the deal King had made with the government, was not surprised by the marshal's decision. Slowly the marchers mounted the bridge and stood side by side in groups of five.

When they were halfway accross the bridge they looked down to the far end. There they saw a line of troopers standing two deep. Major John Cloud stepped forward from among the troopers, a bullhorn in his hand. To Abernathy it looked too much like what the marchers had faced only two days earlier on "Bloody Sunday."

Civil rights marchers faced off against a roadblock of state troopers on March 9, 1965.

"You are ordered to stop and stand where you are," said Cloud through the bullhorn. "This march will not continue."

"We have a right to march," replied King.

When Cloud repeated his order, King asked if he and the marchers could pray where they stood.

"You can have your prayer and then you must return to your church," said Cloud. Abernathy followed King and went down on his knees. Many of the marchers followed suit. Several of the clergy prayed aloud. But as they got up and prepared to return to the chapel, Cloud ordered the troopers to move back.

Abernathy was shocked. The road to Montgomery was clear. This was not part of the compromise. Why had Cloud withdrawn his men? Was it a trap? If the marchers went ahead onto Highway 80, would they be attacked? Or was Wallace trying to make King look like a coward for not going forward when the road was clear? There seemed to be no way of winning.

Abernathy looked at his leader. King shook his head and Abernathy nodded. They turned around and told the others behind them to do the same.

Abernathy knew that there would be younger marchers who would not like this. They might see it as surrendering to the racists. A number of college students who were members of SNCC were already distrustful of King. Abernathy thought this would confirm their belief that King was weak. Then someone in the marching line began to sing "Ain't Gonna Let Nobody Turn Me Around." Others joined in the singing. Abernathy knew from the tone of the voices that they were singing the song with heavy sarcasm. They were indeed being turned around by a man for whom they were rapidly losing respect.

Abernathy turned to look at King. He was grimacing. *He knows*, Abernathy thought. But neither man spoke. They just kept walking back over the bridge.

"AND WE SHALL OVERCOME!"

Many people around the United States began to protest the violent police actions against civil rights marchers in Alabama.

It should have been a day of triumph. King had managed to avoid another bloody confrontation with Alabama's law enforcement. At the same time he had still made his point in the unfinished march. But there were other factors that robbed him of any sense of satisfaction.

Leaders of SNCC, except for the steadfast John Lewis, were unhappy with his refusal to continue the march. They were on the verge of leaving their coalition with the SCLC.

Governor Wallace remained staunchly opposed to any further civil rights march to Montgomery. And, worst of all, more violence had erupted. The previous night, just hours after the march, white racists had attacked several clergymen who had participated in the march. One of the clergymen, James Reeb, a Unitarian minister from Boston, had been seriously injured. Reeb was now hospitalized and in critical condition.

Despite all these difficulties and tragedies, King tried to stay upbeat. Judge Johnson was set to rule on the case for another march within days. Although he had defied the judge's injunction not to march, King was optimistic that Johnson would rule in favor of another march to Montgomery. But now he could only wait. He hoped that the people who had traveled so far would stay in Selma for a third march. Then King got down on his knees and prayed for Reeb, who was clinging to life.

George Wallace

Wallace sat nervously, sinking into a soft sofa while Johnson towered over him in his favorite rocking chair. He felt like a student who had been sent to the principal's office. He had requested the face-to-face meeting with the president, but now he was regretting it. Although both were from the south, Johnson had abandoned the segregationist views that many southern politicians, including Wallace, still held.

Wallace argued that the demonstrators led by King were outsiders. He told Johnson that they only brought trouble and chaos to his state. He expressed sorrow about Reeb, the minister who had died two days earlier from his injuries.

"You know, George," Johnson said, brushing aside Wallace's arguments, "you can turn those demonstrations off in a minute. Why don't you just desegregate all your schools?

You and I go out there in front of those television cameras right now, and you announce you've decided to desegregate every school in Alabama."

"They're locally run," Wallace replied. "I haven't got the political power to do that."

When Johnson pressed him on giving black people the right to register to vote, Wallace again said he didn't have the power.

Johnson leaned in, nose to nose with Wallace. "George, why are you doing this? You came into office a liberal—you spent all your life trying to do things for the poor. Why are you off on this Negro thing? What do you want left after you, when you die? Do you want a great big marble monument that reads, 'George Wallace—He Built'? Or do you want a little piece of pine board that reads, 'George Wallace—He Hated'?"

Wallace didn't have an answer. He was grateful when, after three hours, their talk ended. They went out from the Oval Office to meet reporters and photographers for a press conference in the Rose Garden.

Wallace felt drained, but still his own man. "The president was a gentleman, as he always is," he told the press. "We had a frank and friendly discussion."

When he left the White House later he confided to his aides, "If I'd stayed in there much longer, he'd have had me coming out for civil rights."

President Lyndon Johnson (right) and George Wallace (center) addressed members of the media after meeting privately to discuss events in Selma.

Lyndon Johnson

Chamber of the House of Representatives,
Washington, D.C.,
March 15, 1965, 9:00 p.m.

Johnson did not feel at his best when addressing large groups, as he was about to do now. He did much better in small groups of friends and politicians, where his earthy Texas anecdotes and humor captivated his audience. Here, on a larger stage, he felt the need to be "presidential" in his speeches. Often, that made his language less colorful, effective, and persuasive. But tonight, facing Congress and a television audience of millions, he was determined to be both presidential and compelling. His message demanded it. It would be the first time in 19 years that a president had addressed Congress directly with a legislative message.

Johnson walked up to the podium. He blinked before the bright lights of the TV cameras, looked out at his audience, and began speaking, "At times history and fate meet at a single time in a single place to shape a turning point in man's unending search for freedom. . . . So it was last week in Selma, Alabama."

Martin Luther King Jr.

Selma, Alabama,
March 15, 1965, 9:10 p.m.

King sat hunched over in a chair in a friend's house, surrounded by members of the SCLC. They watched Johnson speak on television. King and the president agreed on the overall campaign for civil rights. But they had not always seen eye to eye on tactics and strategy. The events of the past week in Selma, however, had united the minister and the president. Listening to him tonight, King could not be prouder of Johnson. Then the president announced that in just two days' time he would introduce a voting rights bill before Congress. This bill, he said, would guarantee black people's right to register to vote.

Martin Luther King Jr. (right) and Ralph Abernathy (left)

King led a rousing cheer that filled the room.

"What happened in Selma is part of a far larger movement which reaches into every section and state of America," Johnson continued. "It is not just Negroes but really it is all of us who must overcome the crippling legacy of bigotry and injustice. And—we—shall—overcome!"

As he heard these last words, the slogan of the movement, King was overcome with emotion. He felt a tear trickle down his cheek.

He had been careful to keep his emotions in check in front of his team. Now he didn't care if they saw him cry. This was a turning point in the long years of their struggle. Their cause was no longer just theirs. It was now America's cause. They were alone no longer.

Frank Johnson

Montgomery, Alabama, March 16, 1965

Johnson looked down at the crowded courtroom and called King as his first witness in this hearing. King was proposing another march from Selma to Montgomery for March 21, just five days away. Johnson would decide whether to allow it under the law. The lawyers representing Governor Wallace attacked King in a sharp cross-examination. They tried to get him to admit that he had broken the law by going ahead with his march a week earlier.

Johnson banged his gavel. He told the lawyers that whether what King did was right or wrong was a matter between the judge and King and the marchers.

Then the judge took off his glasses and looked down at King. Johnson asked King if the report was correct that he pulled back after being confronted by the troopers on the March 9 march.

"That is correct," replied King.

"And then did you go forward, or did you turn and go back?" the judge asked.

"We turned around and went back to Selma," King replied.

"And at that point there were no troopers in front of you?" asked the judge.

"That is correct," King replied.

Johnson nodded. The judge was showing Wallace and his racist lawyers that King did not go ahead with the march. It appeared he was free to do so, but he did not. Next, the judge called Lingo, head of the state troopers, to the stand. Johnson did not ask Lingo about his behavior on "Turnaround Tuesday." Instead Johnson asked the trooper about the first attempted march on "Bloody Sunday."

Visibly uncomfortable, Lingo said he was given orders from the governor to restrain the marchers but avoid harming them.

"Regardless of what it meant to do it?" asked the judge.

"No," replied Lingo. "I did not mean to kill them but to use the least force possible to do it."

"Regardless of what it is?" persisted the judge. "Where were you going to stop?"

Lingo explained that he did not mean to use tear gas on the marchers. He said he didn't know who gave the order to do so.

Johnson ended the session saying he would make his decision on the proposed march the following day. Though he sympathized with King, Johnson still felt an obligation to the general population of Alabama. A long march like this could create havoc on the state highway. The marchers' safety, as well as the safety of motorists, was a serious concern. Johnson went home and wrestled with his conscience far into the night. It wasn't easy being a judge, he decided, especially in these turbulent times.

Martin Luther King Jr.

King was ecstatic. Judge Johnson's decision had vindicated him. The judge said that the proposed march to Montgomery reached to the outer limits of what the Constitution allowed. But he also said that the injustice inflicted on Alabama's black citizens by the denial of their voting rights clearly exceeded the limitations. The judge allowed King to go forward with the march. He also ordered Governor Wallace to provide protection along the route from those who might harm the marchers.

King was given some restrictions. There would be no limit on the number of marchers starting out from Selma on the four-lane highway. Once the road was reduced to two lanes, however, by the second day, only 300 marchers could continue. The others could rejoin the march when Highway 80 widened again to four lanes, 24 miles to the east. This time King was determined to follow the letter of the law.

Lynda Blackmon

Selma, Alabama,
March 19, 1965, 7:00 p.m.

Blackmon was the happiest 14-year-old in Selma. Her injuries from "Bloody Sunday" were healing well. The stitches in her head had been removed. The only other reminder of her wounds was a small bandage over her eye. But what made her happy was that she would be among the marchers, the chosen 300, marching to Montgomery in just two days.

At first her father refused to let her go, fearing she might be attacked again. However, the church ladies assured him they would watch over his elder daughter. He finally relented but he did lecture Blackmon. He told her she had to set an example for other young marchers. She reminded him that she would probably be the youngest marcher to go all the way to Montgomery. It was a distinction she bore proudly.

Viola Liuzzo

Thirty-nine-year-old Viola Liuzzo stared at the telephone for a long time. The phone was on a tiny table in the home of the black family where she was staying. Liuzzo was a white housewife from Detroit, Michigan. She was also a member of the National Association for the Advancement of Colored People (NAACP). She had answered King's call for volunteers just days before.

Liuzzo had driven with a few friends from Detroit to Selma in her 1963 blue Oldsmobile. She had left home without saying goodbye to her husband, Anthony, a union leader, or her five children. She was afraid that if she had told Anthony her plans, he would have talked her out of going. But the time had now come for her to make the phone call that she dreaded.

Anthony answered the phone on the first ring. She tried to explain why she had gone to Selma. She wanted to make him understand how important it was for her to do her part against prejudice and bigotry. He told her the march could become violent just as the first march had. She told him that she would not be marching but supporting the marchers by helping provide food and other supplies. She would also transport marchers in her car as needed. This only partly comforted her husband, who was still worried about her safety. She finally told him flatly, "This is something I must do." Then she said she loved him, asked him to hug the children for her, and hung up.

"MARCHING UP TO FREEDOM LAND"

4

Marchers gathered outside Selma's Brown Chapel on the morning of March 21, 1965.

Lynda Blackmon

Brown Chapel, Selma, Alabama,
March 21, 1965, 12:20 p.m.

The crowd at Brown Chapel spilled out into the streets. Blackmon had never seen so many people in one place before. Her head and eye were still bandaged but she felt well enough to march again. Her father was there to see her off. He had her check her knapsack one more time to make sure she had everything she would need. She had a bologna sandwich, cookies, candy, water, and enough clean underwear for three days.

Then, together with hundreds of others, Blackmon listened as King, his wife, Coretta, by his side, addressed the marchers. "March together, children," he boomed. "Don't you get weary, and it will lead us to the Promised Land. And

Alabama will be a new Alabama, and America will be a new America!"

The marchers prepared to leave the chapel and start the long march to Montgomery. Blackmon's father hugged her and told her she'd better mind folks or he would hear about it. Although he tried to hide it, she could tell from his shining eyes that he was proud of her. Then he wished her a happy birthday and left. The next day she would turn 15.

John Lewis

Highway 80, Alabama,
March 21, 1965, 1:05 p.m.

Lewis walked briskly in the front line of the marchers. Nearby were Williams, King and his wife, Coretta, comedian Dick Gregory, and others. When Lewis saw the scene at the other end of the Pettus Bridge, he almost stopped dead in his tracks.

A line of national guardsmen stood at attention. They looked to Lewis like the state troopers who had waited for them only two weeks earlier. But, he had to remind himself, this time it was different. President Johnson had sent in these legions of guardsmen along the route. The guardsmen were there to protect the marchers, not attack them. It was soon clear that the marchers would need protecting.

White people, old and young, lined the roadside, jeering and yelling at the marchers. Some of them held homemade signs with racist slogans. Others drove by in cars and trucks, yelling and cursing at the marchers as they passed.

None of this bothered Lewis. He drew a certain strength from the jeers and yells. They motivated him to keep up the pace. He knew that each passing mile drew the marchers closer to the capitol building in Montgomery. There they would bring their petition to the man most responsible for their problems—Governor George Wallace.

Lewis smiled at the friends on either side of him and joined in the singing that someone had started:

"Keep on walkin', keep on talkin'
Marching up to Freedom Land."

Viola Liuzzo

Highway 80, Alabama,
March 21, 1965, 7:00 p.m.

Liuzzo watched the small group of marchers climb into her Oldsmobile. This was the third run she had made between Selma and the marchers' evening destination, 7 miles from Selma. She was transporting marchers who weren't part of the chosen 300 who could continue under Judge Johnson's order.

Those who would stay the night were setting up four big tents on a farm. The thousand or so people who voluntarily left the march had mostly gone back to Selma. Many had ridden in buses and a train chartered by the Justice Department.

But there were so many of them that volunteers with cars were needed to transport people too.

Liuzzo enjoyed the drive. She listened with rapt attention to the marchers' stories of what they had experienced. She felt part of the march, part of a family of activists fighting for a cause that was just. She had never felt more alive, more joyful, in her life.

Another group of passengers climbed in and the back door of her Oldsmobile slammed shut. She started up the car and headed back down the darkening highway to Selma.

Lynda Blackmon
Highway 80, Alabama,
March 21, 1965, 9:00 p.m.

Seven miles, Blackmon thought. *That's how far we've walked since leaving Selma.*

The adults said they'd have to cover many more miles to reach Montgomery in five days.

A farmer named David Hall and his wife were good enough to welcome the marchers onto their 80-acre farm. So the marchers had pitched their four big tents on farmland for the night. Local church people provided a dinner of spaghetti and meat sauce for the marchers. Food had never tasted so good to Blackmon.

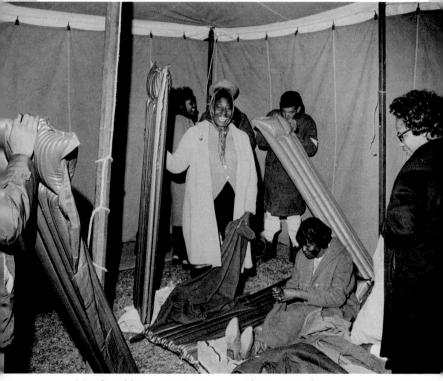

Marchers blew up air mattresses as they prepared their camp for the night.

She crawled into her sleeping bag, but was far too excited to sleep. She reviewed the day's march in her mind. She thought about the singing and the talking. The jeering and mean words of the people in the passing cars came back to her. A seasoned marcher, she was used to ignoring this sort of thing when it happened.

There were about 2,000 marchers staying the night. Tomorrow all but 300 would have to return to Selma as Judge Johnson had ordered. Blackmon felt the march would be very different in the morning with so few marchers. She was glad she had older friends and the church ladies there to watch out for her. Tomorrow was her birthday, but she didn't expect a cake or a party. She didn't need that. The march itself was the best birthday present she could imagine. And with such thoughts in her head, she drifted off into a deep sleep.

John Lewis

Lewis climbed out of the car and thanked the driver. He was back with the march after a night in Selma. It bothered him that he had to return there each night of the march. The doctors who treated his fractured skull didn't want him sleeping on the ground but in a proper bed. It bothered him and yet he was grateful he was still well enough to be part of this historic occasion.

As King and other marchers greeted Lewis, someone handed him an orange vest. All the marchers were given them to help guardsmen identify them as they marched. Such precautions were necessary now that they had left Dallas County and were entering Lowndes County. Lowndes was likely to be an even greater hotbed of racial hatred than any place the marchers had yet encountered.

As he fell in step with the others, Lewis could feel the sun hot on his neck, making him sweat.

It had become quite warm for March. Lewis looked skyward and saw helicopters piloted by guardsmen overhead whirling about. They were looking out for snipers who might fire on the marchers from the tops of buildings and hillsides.

Amid the helicopters, Lewis suddenly saw a small plane appear. The words *Confederate Air Force* were written on the plane's side. As it flew above them, the air filled with sheets of paper. As the sheets floated down, he could see that they were leaflets. Lewis grabbed one and looked at it. It was filled with hateful racist propaganda.

Lewis crumpled the leaflet in his fist, threw it to the ground, and picked up his pace.

Martin Luther King Jr.

Highway 80, Alabama,
March 22, 1965, 9:00 p.m.

King took off his shoes and rubbed his aching feet. Coretta smiled.

"Do you think your feet will make it to Montgomery?" she asked her husband.

"I hope so," he replied.

The question, though said in jest, bothered him. She knew he would be leaving the march tomorrow to fly to Cleveland, Ohio.

John Lewis (left), Martin Luther King Jr. (center) and Ralph Abernathy (right, reading newspaper) led marchers on the way to Montgomery.

There he would receive an award and make a speech. He would rejoin the marchers on the last day before they reached Montgomery. He didn't want to leave them, but it was important that he continue to speak out. An important part of his work was to communicate with all those Americans who supported civil rights across the country.

"You look tired," Coretta told him. "You should get some sleep."

"Not yet," he told her. "I'm going to take a walk around the camp and talk to people. That's the least I can do before I have to leave the march."

He put his shoes back on and got up. He walked out into the camp, limping slightly from the blisters on his feet.

Lynda Blackmon

Highway 80, Alabama,
March 23, 1965, 10:15 a.m.

Blackmon pulled her orange poncho tighter around her shoulders as she slogged through the pouring rain. The marchers had been chilled the first day, burned by the sun the second, and now were marching through a downpour.

The landscape through which they were passing was just as gloomy as the weather. It was swampy and boggy. But the local black people they passed lifted their spirits. Many greeted the marchers with smiles and warm words of encouragement. Some of these locals actually dropped what they were doing and joined the march.

Blackmon was grateful for the locals who showed kindness, and for the national guardsmen. The guardsmen made the passing cars and trucks move quickly, not allowing the people inside them time to jeer and yell at the marchers. By the time the marchers reached the night's campsite, most of the locals had left and headed home.

Blackmon wished she had a warm home to go to for the night. Still, she was thankful to be able to wash the grit and mud off of herself at a nearby house. Then she returned to one of the tents and laid down in her sleeping bag. A layer of straw and a plastic tarp protected her from the mud. Unlike the first night, she had no trouble falling asleep. She, like most of the other marchers, was bone tired and ready for a good rest.

"THERE NEVER WAS A MOMENT ... MORE HONORABLE"

5

Coretta Scott King (center right) helped lead the marchers on the road to Montgomery.

John Lewis

John Lewis walked with a spring in his step. It was hot and noisy. His face was sunburnt and his feet were sore. But nothing could ruin his sunny mood. The marchers were almost at the end of their journey and the city of Montgomery was almost in sight. As the afternoon wore on, more and more people joined the march.

On the widened highway, Judge Johnson's order restricting the number of marchers had been lifted. They had grown from 300 to what looked like thousands. They included entertainers and celebrities, some of whom had been persuaded to come by King's good friend, singer and actor Harry Belafonte. Lewis could see the steeple of the church at the City of St. Jude. This Catholic complex had been built to help serve the black community. It consisted of a church, a hospital, and a school. Lewis grinned.

He wouldn't be going back to Selma tonight. He'd have a bed to sleep in right here in Montgomery.

Viola Liuzzo

St. Jude's Hospital, Montgomery, Alabama, March 24, 1965, 6:00 p.m.

Liuzzo was tired after sleeping in her car the night before. She had given up her cot in the complex to a marcher who'd arrived early. Now she was in charge of the hospital's first-aid station, ready to treat marchers with blistered feet or heat stroke.

She asked them about the day's journey. She was beginning to regret that she had not marched, but she knew she was needed as a driver. She was comforted with the knowledge that the following morning she too would be in front of the state capitol. She would join the marchers in witnessing a historic moment. They would listen to the speeches of many of the march leaders, but especially her hero, Martin Luther King.

She'd heard he had only arrived at St. Jude's a short time before the marchers, having flown in from Cleveland. She hoped to see and hear him tonight when the marchers came together for the scheduled concert.

Lynda Blackmon

City of St. Jude, Montgomery, Alabama, March 24, 1965, 6:15 p.m.

As she reached the St. Jude complex, Blackmon fell to the ground and cried. She had done it. The youngest of the marchers, she had come through with the best of them. Tomorrow she would join the others at the state capitol, just 6 miles away.

One of the first people she saw as she arrived was her sister, Joanne. Her father had driven Joanne over to surprise Blackmon. Joanne said their father had driven back to Selma. He had gone to pick up more people who wanted to join the last leg of the march.

As Blackmon told Joanne about her experiences over the past four days, she could hear music in the distance. The many entertainers and singers among the marchers were getting ready for the big concert that would take place that evening. She only hoped her father would return in time to enjoy the concert with them.

Viola Liuzzo

City of St. Jude, Montgomery, Alabama, March 25, 1965, 8:00 a.m.

Last night had been a late one, full of music, comedy, and speeches. Liuzzo had enjoyed every minute of it. The musicians included folk singers Pete Seeger; Joan Baez; and Peter, Paul, and Mary. Pop singers Sammy Davis Jr., Tony Bennett, and Johnny Mathis had also performed. No one had gotten much sleep but they all had risen early to finish their triumphant march to Montgomery. This time Liuzzo and the other volunteers would join them.

Now she and one of St. Jude's priests, Father Tim Deasy, watched the march begin. She asked Deasy if he knew a place where they could get a better view of the departing marchers. He smiled and led her to the church tower. There they watched the long line of marchers wind down the road toward the capital.

Liuzzo looked down in awe. She was happy, but her happiness was marred by a strange feeling. As they descended the steps of the tower, she shared her fears with Deasy.

"Something is going to happen today," she said. "I feel it. Somebody is going to get killed."

The priest tried to reassure her that the idea was nonsense. The march had been relatively peaceful and he didn't believe anything would happen to change that.

"I feel it," she persisted. "Somebody is going to get killed. You know, it might even be Governor Wallace himself—he may be killed by one of his own because he has lots of enemies down here. And they'd lay the blame on the marchers."

Then, before joining the marchers, Liuzzo went into the church. She asked God to prevent whatever terrible thing was going to happen.

Coretta Scott King

Montgomery, Alabama,
March 25, 1965, 11:30 a.m.

Walking through downtown Montgomery with her husband, Coretta Scott King felt she was taking a stroll down memory lane. They passed the Dexter Avenue Baptist Church, her husband's first congregation. That was where they had started the Montgomery bus boycott back in 1955. Had 10 years passed since then? It didn't seem possible. Then again, so much had changed for black Americans in that time. So many things were still changing.

Rosa Parks was right there, marching alongside them. Parks was the courageous woman who had sparked the bus boycott. She had refused to give up her seat in the back of a Montgomery bus and the rest was history.

King was glad to see so many other friends and colleagues from the movement surrounding them. As she took her husband's hand, the Capitol Building came into sight. Their journey was nearly over.

George Wallace

Capitol Building, Montgomery, Alabama, March 25, 1965, 12:00 p.m.

Wallace peered cautiously out the window of his executive secretary's office at the massive crowds gathered below. It had not been a good week for the governor. He had tried, with little success, to find ways he could make the marchers look bad. The national media had, much to his distress, described them as heroes and cast him as the leading villain.

About 15 marchers, all Alabama residents, had tried to enter the capitol building to present him with a petition demanding voting rights. But he gave the guards downstairs orders not to let them in. And he had no intention of going out to meet them. He had thought about closing the capitol for the day. Instead, he declared it a holiday for all female state employees. He justified the holiday by claiming that female employees might be molested by the male marchers.

Outside, the march leaders began to make their speeches. Wallace decided it was time to leave and sneaked out through a back door. He learned later that he had left just in time. When he got back to the governor's mansion he received an update from a capitol employee. He was told the marchers' Alabama delegation convinced the guards to let them into the building soon after he left.

Frank Johnson

Montgomery, Alabama,
March 25, 1965, 12:00 p.m.

Judge Johnson looked out the window of the office of his friend, Judge Richard Rives. Johnson felt a sense of satisfaction as thousands of marchers gathered in front of the state capitol.

Rives looked at the satisfied expression on Johnson's face and said with good humor, "This does indeed reach the outer perimeters of what is constitutionally allowed."

"Yes, indeed," said Johnson, with a wink.

Martin Luther King Jr.

Montgomery, Alabama,
March 25, 1965, 12:30 p.m.

King looked out at the thousands upon thousands of people gathered in the square before the capitol building. He never dreamed so many people would come to Montgomery to see the march's triumphant finish. The marchers had failed to bring their petition before Governor Wallace, but that was only a minor disappointment now. With the Voting Rights Act before Congress, they had bypassed the governor and his segregationist agenda. Once Congress passed the bill, Wallace would be powerless to stop black Alabamians from registering to vote.

Martin Luther King Jr. addressed the crowd outside the Alabama state capitol building on March 25, 1965. He said, "There never was a moment in American history more honorable and more inspiring than the pilgrimage of clergymen and laymen of every race and faith pouring into Selma to face danger at the side of its embattled Negroes."

Now it was time to celebrate their victory with words. King began speaking into the microphones. "I stand before you this afternoon with the conviction that segregation is on its deathbed in Alabama, and the only thing uncertain about it is how costly the segregationists and Wallace will make the funeral. . . . I know some of you are asking today, 'How long will it take?'. . . It will not be long. Because truth crushed to earth will rise again. How long? Not long, because no lie can live forever. . . . How long? Not long, because mine eyes have seen the glory of the coming of the Lord!"

The crowd roared as he quoted the lyrics of "The Battle Hymn of the Republic." They had truly, King decided, won the battle, but the war was not over. Not yet.

Viola Liuzzo

Highway 80, Alabama,
March 25, 1965, 8:00 p.m.

It had been a long and eventful day and one that Liuzzo would never forget. Once the rally at the capitol building had ended, she returned to work—transporting marchers back to Selma in her Oldsmobile. Having just dropped off a carload at Brown Chapel, she was now heading back to Montgomery.

Leroy Moton, a 19-year-old black activist who had shared the driving, rode beside her. She enjoyed Moton's company. It gave her someone to talk to on the lonely drive through the evening.

They were singing when a red and white Impala pulled alongside them at a traffic light. Inside were four white men. They didn't look friendly. Liuzzo sped forward, breaking one of the rules for volunteer drivers: don't exceed the speed limit and attract attention.

Leroy Moton

But Liuzzo wanted to get away from the men in the Impala as quickly as possible.

She glanced in the rear window and saw, to her distress, that the Impala was behind her and coming on fast. It brushed up twice against her rear bumper. "These white folks are crazy," she told Moton.

Before Moton could reply, the Impala pulled up alongside them. Liuzzo looked out her window and saw one of the passengers pointing a gun directly at her. It was the last thing she saw.

Leroy Moton

Highway 80, Alabama,
March 25, 1965, 8:05 p.m.

Moton screamed as gunshots erupted from the Impala. Four, five, six. Liuzzo slumped onto his shoulder, her head spurting blood. The car veered sharply off the road. He grabbed for the wheel and stomped his foot down on the brake. But the

Viola Liuzzo was shot through
the window of her car.

car flew into a ditch and came to an abrupt stop
on an embankment.

Moton was in a daze as he shut off the ignition
and shook Liuzzo. She fell to one side in the seat,
blood oozing from two holes in her head. It was
clear that she was dead.

Looking up, Moton saw the other car turn
around and approach them again. Instinctively,
he lay down and played dead. He heard the car
pull up and the hushed voices of the men inside.

He didn't move a muscle. He held his breath as long as he could, trying to keep still. Finally, the car started up again and pulled away. It felt like the longest minute of Moton's life.

He waited another couple of minutes before allowing himself to move. Finally, he pulled himself up. He looked back and forth along the dark highway, searching for the headlights of approaching cars. As one after another sped past, he honked the horn, but no one stopped.

Moton scrambled out of the car and began trying to wave down someone, anyone. He was running now, in a full panic. His feet carried him down the highway in the direction of Montgomery.

Finally, a truck approached. He ran into the middle of the road, waving his arms and yelling. The driver stopped. Moton was relieved to see the truck was full of civil rights workers. He climbed into the truck's cab, told the workers what had happened, and promptly passed out.

Coretta Scott King

Atlanta, Georgia,
March 25, 1965, 9:30 p.m.

The Kings stepped into the crowded airport. They had just flown back to Atlanta from Montgomery. Coretta Scott King had enjoyed the march and was grateful to have shared this experience with her husband. Too often commitments and other demands kept them separate. But now she was happy to be back home.

Martin looked tired but happy. As they crossed the airport, a voice came on the loudspeaker paging him for a phone call. He sighed and excused himself and went to the nearest phone to answer it. He returned a few minutes later, his face ashen, his eyes dead.

"What was it?" she asked.

"We are in for a season of suffering I told them in my speech today," he said. "For all our triumphs there would still be a season of suffering. But I had not expected it so soon."

87

She was deeply concerned now. "What is it? What happened?"

Then he told her about Liuzzo's murder.

Lyndon Johnson

Johnson was on the phone with J. Edgar Hoover, head of the Federal Bureau of Investigation (FBI). Hoover hated King with a passion and believed that all civil rights activists were communists, a group he considered to be enemies of the United States. He was not a man with whom Johnson relished dealing. But this morning he was grateful for Hoover's call.

Hoover told the president that the FBI was arresting the four men responsible for the killing of Viola Liuzzo. They were all from Birmingham, Alabama, and members of the racist Ku Klux Klan group.

Johnson was impressed by the swiftness of the arrests. "How in the devil did you find them so fast?" he asked.

"It was easy, Mr. President," boasted Hoover. "One of the four men in that car was a long-time FBI informant. He called us soon after the shooting."

"Good work," said Johnson. "It's just too bad he couldn't have done something to stop them from killing that poor woman."

"THE VOTE IS THE MOST POWERFUL INSTRUMENT EVER DEVISED BY MAN"

6

President Lyndon Johnson and Martin Luther King Jr. shook hands on August 6, 1965 after Johnson signed the Voting Rights Act.

John Lewis

To Lewis, it seemed a dream to be sitting in the Oval Office. He was just a few feet away from the president of the United States. The feeling that this was unreal was heightened by all that he had been through in the past six months. The visit with Johnson, which included several other civil rights leaders, lasted 20 minutes. His long legs stretched out across a chair and his hands folded behind his head, the president dominated the meeting. Johnson talked about all that they had achieved through the Selma marches. Later today he would sign the Voting Rights Act for which they had all worked so hard.

As the meeting was winding down, Johnson leaned his large frame toward Lewis and said, "Now John, you've got to go back and get all those folks registered. You've got to go back and get those boys." It was clear to Lewis that "the boys" the president was referring to were the southern white racists. They were the southern white racists who had done everything they could to stop black people from registering to vote. Lewis promised Johnson that he would get them.

Lyndon Johnson

Capitol Building, Washington, D.C.,
August 6, 1965, 11:35 a.m.

Johnson waited to enter the Capitol Rotunda. He reviewed what might be one of the most important speeches of his presidency. Today, Johnson would sign a law that would secure the right to vote for all black Americans. The Senate had passed the bill only two days before, and the House of Representatives the day before that.

"The President of the United States!" called out the Sergeant at Arms of the Senate.

Johnson entered to loud applause and stepped up to the podium. He looked out at the sea of faces, which included nearly every member of Congress. Also present were members of the Supreme Court and invited guests, including King. Johnson cleared his throat and began to speak.

"Today is a triumph for freedom as huge as any victory that has ever been won on any battlefield. Yet to seize the meaning of this day, we must recall darker times. . . .

"Today we strike away the last major shackle of those fierce and ancient bonds of slavery. Today the Negro story and the American story fuse and blend. . . .

"So, let me now say to every Negro in this country: You must register. You must vote. . . . Your future, and your children's future, depends upon it. . . .

"If you do this, then you will find . . . that the vote is the most powerful instrument ever devised by man for breaking down injustice and destroying the terrible walls which imprison men because they are different from other men."

Martin Luther King Jr.

Capitol Building, Washington, D.C.,
August 6, 1965, 12:05 p.m.

King stood watching the president with nearly a hundred other people, including Rosa Parks and John Lewis. Johnson sat at his desk and chose one of the dozens of fountain pens laid out before him. This was a moment for which King had been waiting for many years. It was a moment he was sure would live in history. It was in this very room that President Lincoln had signed the Emancipation Proclamation 102 years before. The previous day King had spent an hour alone with Johnson.

Both had deep respect and appreciation for the other. Both realized that without the other they could not have accomplished both the Civil Rights Act and now the Voting Rights Act. Despite their moments of tension and disagreement, they had been an effective team.

King watched, fascinated, as Johnson made one tiny curve of a letter in his signature. Then he picked up another pen to continue.

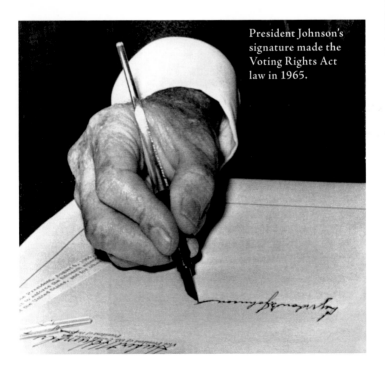

President Johnson's signature made the Voting Rights Act law in 1965.

He made another little jot, and then he picked up yet another pen. King knew the reason for this strange way of writing. Each one of the pens Johnson used to sign the act was a historic memento. After the ceremony the pens would be distributed to many of the people gathered around the desk. As the president finished his signature with a flourish, the gathered assembly applauded. He began to hand the pens out to people. Parks got one and so did Lewis. Then Johnson looked at King. "Dr. King," he said, "you have earned this many times over."

"And so have you, Mr. President," replied King.

The men shook hands. The struggle for civil rights was not over. Still, King felt that it would end in victory, a victory from which all Americans—black and white—would benefit.

U.S. Army MPs (military police) guarded
marchers on the road to Montgomery.

EPILOGUE

The passing of the Voting Rights Act finally gave black people the power of the vote. Between August 10 and August 31, 1965, more than 27,000 African Americans registered to vote for the first time in the South.

Within two months black voters in the South numbered more than 56,000. Within a year, there were 9,000 newly registered black voters in Dallas County, Alabama. The power of these new voters was displayed when they helped vote Sheriff Jim Clark out of office in 1966.

Martin Luther King Jr. continued to fight for civil rights for black people as well as for all poor Americans. He went to Memphis, Tennessee, to participate in a garbage workers' strike in April 1968. On April 4, an assassin's bullet killed King on the balcony of the Lorraine Motel where he was staying. King's legacy lives on today.

Ralph Abernathy became president of the SCLC after King's assassination. He led the

Civil Rights marchers crossed the Edmund
Pettus Bridge in March 1965.

Poor People's March on Washington, D.C., just a month after King's death. He resigned as president of SCLC in 1977 and ran unsuccessfully for a congressional seat in Georgia. Abernathy returned to full-time ministry in Atlanta and died there on April 17, 1990, at the age of 64.

John Lewis left SNCC in 1966. He joined the Field Foundation, which supports community empowerment through justice, art, and leadership investment. He then became director of the Voter Education Project. In 1981 he was elected to the Atlanta City Council. In 1987 he was elected to Congress from Georgia's Fifth District, an office he still holds today. In 2013 Lewis wrote *March: Book One*. The book is the first in a trilogy of graphic novels telling about his experiences in the Civil Rights Movement.

Coretta Scott King founded the Martin Luther King Jr. Center for Nonviolent Social Change in Atlanta in 1968. She served as the center's first president and chief executive. She died in Mexico following a heart attack and stroke on January 30, 2006, at the age of 78.

President Lyndon Johnson continued passing laws to help needy Americans. His Great Society programs helped the poor and the elderly. They included Head Start, which helped poor children get a "head start" in education and Medicare and Medicaid, which provided health care to millions of elderly and low-income Americans. But his pursuit of war against communists in Vietnam proved unpopular and eventually cost the lives of 58,000 U.S. soldiers. As a result Johnson did not run for reelection in 1968. He retired to his Texas ranch and died there at age 64 of a heart attack on January 22, 1973.

George Wallace served four nonconsecutive terms as governor of Alabama, more than any other governor in that state. While campaigning for president in 1972, Wallace was shot. He survived the shooting but was paralyzed from the waist down and confined to a wheelchair. He later apologized for his earlier stand on segregation and befriended black voters, many of whom supported him as governor. He died of heart failure on September 13, 1998, at age 79.

After losing his position as sheriff, Jim Clark got a job selling mobile homes. In 1978 he was convicted of smuggling marijuana and served nine months in prison. He died in 2007 at age 84.

Judge Frank Johnson continued to fight for the cause of civil rights. In the 1970s he helped to reform the Alabama prison system. President Bill Clinton awarded him the Presidential Medal of Freedom in 1995. Johnson died at age 80 on July 23, 1999, in Montgomery. The courthouse in which he served was renamed in his honor.

Viola Liuzzo's funeral was held on March 30, 1965. King was among the attendees. Liuzzo remains the only white woman known to have been murdered during the civil rights movement.

In 1991 women of the SCLC placed a marker on the place along Highway 80 where she was killed.

The three men accused of killing Liuzzo went on trial in May 1965. The trial ended in a hung jury because the jurors could not agree on the men's guilt or innocence.

A memorial stone marks the place where Viola Liuzzo was killed.

Collie Leroy Wilkins, the man who was accused of shooting Liuzzo, was acquitted in a second trial in October. Judge Frank Johnson oversaw a third trial in November and pressured the jury to turn in a verdict of guilty. The three men were convicted of violating Liuzzo's civil rights. Johnson imposed the maximum sentence of 10 years for Wilkins and the other two Klansmen.

Leroy Moton left Selma soon after Liuzzo's murder for fear he too would be killed by Klansmen. He eventually moved to Hartford, Connecticut, where he still lives today. He regularly visits schools to tell the story of the night of the murder. He also talks to students about his role in the Selma march.

Lynda Blackmon Lowery still lives in Selma and works as a case manager at a mental health center there. In 2015 she wrote a book about her experiences on the march, *Turning 15 on the Road to Freedom*.

Civil Rights marchers
outside of the Alabama
State Capitol on
March 25, 1965.

TIMELINE

March 7, 1965

4:00 p.m. Some 500 marchers leave Brown Chapel in Selma, Alabama, to begin a 54-mile march to the capitol in Montgomery

4:15 p.m. On the Edmund Pettus Bridge, state troopers and the sheriff's posse stop marchers and use clubs, whips, and tear gas to brutally attack them, ending the march

March 8

9:00 a.m. Federal Court Judge Frank Johnson rules on a temporary injunction for a second march that Martin Luther King Jr. is planning from Selma to Montgomery

March 9

1:30 p.m. The second march to Montgomery begins, but when again faced by troopers, King turns and leads the marchers back to Brown Chapel

8:00 p.m. James Reeb, a Unitarian minister from Boston and a member of the march, is brutally attacked by white racists on a Selma street and seriously injured

March 11

James Reeb dies in the hospital

March 13

Noon Alabama Governor George Wallace meets with President Johnson at the White House for a three-hour meeting. Johnson attempts to persuade Wallace to allow the next march from Selma to proceed peacefully and give up his pro-segregation position

MARCH 16

10:00 A.M. Judge Johnson rules in favor of King's third march to Montgomery

MARCH 21

The third and final Selma march, led by King, begins with more than 3,000 marchers

MARCH 22

With their numbers reduced by agreement to 300, the marchers cover 14 miles

MARCH 24

6:00 P.M. At the end of their last full day on the road, the marchers, their numbers swelled to 5,000, arrive at the City of St. Jude, a Catholic Church complex a few miles outside of Montgomery

MARCH 25

NOON The marchers arrive at the Capitol building in Montgomery. Governor Wallace refuses to see them and King gives a riveting speech

8:00 P.M. On her way to pick up marchers and bring them back to Selma, Klansmen in a car that had been following her shoot white civil rights activist Viola Liuzzo, killing her

AUGUST 6

12:05 P.M. President Johnson signs the Voting Rights Act, guaranteeing the right to register to vote for all Americans, including black people in the South

GLOSSARY

bigotry (BIH-guh-tree)—treating someone of a different religious, racial, or ethnic group with hatred or intolerance

complex (kahm-PLEKS)—a group of related buildings with a common function or purpose

detrimental (deh-trih-MEN-tuhl)—harmful

injunction (in-JUHNK-shuhn)—a legal action that requires someone to do or not do something while a judge gathers facts about an issue

Ku Klux Klan (KOO KLUHX KLAN)—a group that promoted hate against African Americans, Catholics, Jews, immigrants, and other groups

media (MEE-dee-uh)—TV, radio, newspapers, and other communication forms that send out messages to large groups of people

petition (puh-TISH-uhn)—a letter signed by many people asking leaders for a change

plaintiff (PLANE-tif)—person or group of people who file the complaint in a lawsuit

poncho (PAHN-cho)—a waterproof garment with a hood

posse (POSS-ee)—a group of people gathered together by law enforcement leaders to take action such as catching a criminal

propaganda (praw-puh-GAN-duh)—information spread to try to influence the thinking of people; often not completely true or fair

sanction (SANGK-shun)—to officially approve or support

segregation (seg-ruh-GAY-shuhn)—practice of separating people of different races, income classes, or ethnic groups

CRITICAL THINKING QUESTIONS

1. The Selma March was actually three separate marches. Why was each march important, and how did each lead to the next one and the passing of the Voting Rights Act later that year?

2. Martin Luther King Jr. felt bad about the secret deal he made with authorities about the "Turnaround Tuesday" march. What might have happened if he had not turned around and ended the march? Do you think he made the right decision? Why or why not?

3. Martin Luther King Jr. and President Lyndon Johnson worked together to secure voting rights for African Americans in the South. Why could one not have achieved success without the other? What did each of them bring to their partnership that helped to achieve their goal?

INTERNET SITES

Use FactHound to find Internet sites related to this book.

Visit *www.facthound.com*

Just type in 9781515779414 and go.

FURTHER READING

Aretha, David. *The Story of the Selma Voting Rights Marches in Photographs.* Berkeley Heights, N.J.: Enslow, 2014.

Burgan, Michael. *The Voting Rights Acts of 1965: An Interactive History Adventure.* Mankato, Minn.: Capstone Press, 2015.

Lewis, John. *March: Book One.* Marietta, Ga.: Top Shelf Productions, 2013.

Lowery, Lynda Blackmon. *Turning 15 on the Road to Freedom: My Story of the 1965 Selma Voting Rights March.* New York: Dial Books, 2015.

SELECTED BIBLIOGRAPHY

Branch, Taylor. *The King Years: Historic Moments in the Civil Rights Movement*. New York: Simon & Schuster, 2013.

Fager, Charles E. *Selma 1965: The March That Changed The South*. New York: Charles Scribner's Sons, 1974.

Frady, Marshall. *Martin Luther King, Jr.* New York: Viking Penguin, 2002.

Lesher, Stephan. *George Wallace: American Populist*. New York: Addison-Wesley, 1994.

King, Coretta Scott. *My Life with Martin Luther King, Jr.* New York: Henry Holt, 1993 [revised edition].

Kotz, Nick. *Judgment Days: Lyndon Baines Johnson, Martin Luther King Jr., and the Laws that Changed America*. Boston: Houghton Mifflin, 2005.

Lewis, David Levering. *King: A Biography*. Urbana: University of Illinois Press, 2013.

Lewis, John. *Walking with the Wind: A Memoir of the Movement*. New York: Simon & Schuster, 1998.

Oates, Stephen B. "The Week The World Watched Selma." *American Heritage*, June/July 1982, pp. 48–63.

INDEX

ABOUT THE AUTHOR

Steven Otfinoski has written more than 190 books for young readers. His previous titles in the Tangled History series include books on the Underground Railroad, the attack on Pearl Harbor, and the assassination of President Kennedy. Three of his nonfiction books have been named Books for the Teen Age by the New York Public Library. He lives in Connecticut with his wife.